THE BULLY

Invisible Hope Series Book 4

Print information available on the last page

Rev. date: 03/10/2017

To order additional copies of this book, contact:
Xlibris
1-888-795-4274
www.Xlibris.com
Orders@Xlibris.com

THE BULLY

Invisible Hope Series Book 4

MARSHA FRANKS

Illustrated by: Elenei Rae Pulido

"I told ya to give me that candy bar!" Bobby yelled as he shoved Jacob to the ground.

"Here," Jacob whined. "Just leave me alone."

'You're just a big baby!" Bobby said as he walked away tearing the wrapper off the candy bar.

Again at school, Bobby Carter is being mean to another student. His teacher, Mrs. Shaw, has scolded Bobby for his behavior, but he just ignores her. Mrs. Shaw suspects Bobby has problems at home with his Dad. She saw red marks on his arm once and asked Bobby if his dad had hit him, but Bobby insisted he fell and was not hit by his dad. She has not seen red marks on him again, but sometimes he will wear a long sleeve shirt on a warm day. Mrs. Shaw does not know of any other family members Bobby could live with or she would have already called authorities about her suspicions. She doesn't want him going to a foster home. Bobby needs someone to love him and care for him. He is just a child that needs nurturing.

Bobby's mom left home about 3 years ago when Bobby was 5. He lives with his Dad, Bart Carter. Bart has a reputation for drinking a lot, and being angry all the time since his wife left. Cecelia Carter left because she couldn't take the abuse from Bart anymore. Bobby understands why his mom left, but doesn't understand why she left him there. Cecelia didn't think Bart would be abusive to his own son, so she got away before Bart hurt her so bad she couldn't go.

It is getting close to Thanksgiving. The holidays are hard for Bobby because his dad drinks more during this time of year.

"Bobby, get up!" Bart yelled at his son. "It's Saturday, you've got to do the laundry!"

"Ok Dad", Bobby said. Bobby gets up and gets dressed. He goes to the kitchen and fixes himself some cereal for breakfast. His dad is sitting on the back porch drinking out of a liquor bottle.

'Oh no', Bobby thought, 'He's started early. I need to stay out of Dad's way today.'

Later, Bobby got the washer going and cleaned up the dishes in the kitchen before his dad yelled at him about it. Bobby feels more like a maid than a son, from having to do all the chores around the house. While finishing up in the kitchen, his Dad comes in the back door. Bart stumbles and falls inside the door.

Bobby ran over to him and asked, "Dad, are you ok?" No matter how his dad treats him, Bobby knows his dad is all he has.

"I'm fine!" Dad yelled. "Just leave me alone!" As he got up he shoved Bobby so hard, he fell to the floor. Bart stumbled into the living room and fell on the couch, closing his eyes and putting his feet up over the arm.

Bobby got up and ran to his room, shutting the door. He lay on his bed and cried, wishing his mom was there.

'Why would mom leave me here?' he thought. 'Why does she not love me? Why does my dad have to be so mean? Why do I have to live here?' Bobby had so many questions. His life is more about him taking care of his Dad than his Dad taking care of him. He is alone and very unhappy.

'I'll run away', Bobby thought. 'My Dad won't care if I'm gone anyway, except for someone to wait on him.'

He cried as he tried to think of some place he could go where he'd be safe from his dad. He could not think of anywhere he could go. He has no friends and no other family. He has no place to go where he could live and be happy.

"Mom!" he cried into his folded arms. "Mom, please come and get me, I miss you. I want to be with you, Mom."

"What are you cryin' for, you little sissy girl!" Bart yelled as he opened Bobby's bedroom door. "Shut up now and fix me a sandwich!"

Bobby slid off his bed and ran towards the kitchen, trying to dry his tears on the way there. He fixed his Dad a sandwich and poured him a glass of tea, even though he knew his Dad wouldn't drink it.

"It's ready Dad!" Bobby called.

Bart stumbled into the kitchen and sat at the table in front of his sandwich.

"You want anything else Dad?" Bobby asked.

"You get them clothes done?"

"Yeah." Bobby replied.

"Ok, just leave me alone." Bart told him.

Bobby went back to his room and lay on his bed. His thoughts went back to running away. 'Mom', he thought. 'Where are you?'

A few days later, Bobby is in his room and turns over in his bed. He could hear his dad moving around and getting ready for work, so he gets up and gets dressed. Walking into the kitchen, his dad is finishing his coffee and is fixing himself a sandwich for his lunchbox.

Bart sees his son and said, "Why didn't you get up and fix my lunch? All you do is eat and sleep...you're good for nothin'...there's no meat left for you a sandwich. You can just take some bread for your lunch."

"Dad, I get hungry at school." Bobby whispered to him.

"You get hungry!" his dad yelled as he walked towards Bobby. "I work to pay for a roof over your head, get you some food, and you complain!"

Bobby backed up, but not before his dad could strike him across the face. Bart still smelled of alcohol from drinking the night before.

"You better be glad you got what you have! Your momma left you here for me to take care of you. She ran off and probably has someone taking care of her that has lots of money. She doesn't want you, so you've got to stay here and help me. I'm goin' to work. You better get off to school." Bart went out the door.

Bobby went to the bathroom and washed the blood off his lip where his dad hit him. Tears rolled down his face as he thought about what his dad just said.

'Does my mom not love me?' he thought. "It must be true cause she left me here.'

Bobby walked to school. As he sits in the classroom, his stomach is growling. There was no cereal or milk left this morning. This is Friday and his dad gets groceries when he gets off work on Friday's after he gets paid. Dad usually gets bread, milk, cereal, sandwich meat, peanut butter, some canned items and cigarettes. The groceries have to last all week till his dad gets paid again the next Friday. But his dad also gets alcohol to drink. He often goes during the week to get more of that.

It is break time at school. Bobby sees Tommy Brown get some crackers and a coke from the machines in the break area. He is hungry and he knows all he has for lunch is bread. He goes up to Tommy and says, "Give me that stuff, Tommy!" and Bobby grabs it out of Tommy's hands. Tommy is smaller than Bobby and runs off towards the classroom. Mrs. Shaw comes out of the classroom looking for Bobby, and sees him at the end of the hallway. Bobby has already shoved all the crackers in his mouth and is finishing the coke.

"Bobby." Mrs. Shaw said to him. "Bobby, you cannot keep on taking the other children's snacks from them. Do I need to go talk to your father?"

"No, Mrs. Shaw. Don't go see my Father, it would just make him mad at me." Bobby said as he hung his head.

"Bobby, do you have food at home?" she asked.

"Yes." Bobby replied. "But it's not as good as the snacks at school. My dad doesn't give me money for snacks." He did not tell Mrs. Shaw that they didn't have money for his snacks or very much food.

"Well, Bobby, you need to bring your own snacks and stop taking them from the other children." Mrs. Shaw said.

"Ok." Bobby said. But he knew if he wanted a good snack, the only way he would get one is to take it from the other children. Any extra money his dad had went to buy himself more alcohol.

Mrs. Shaw looked at Bobby and shook her head, not knowing what she should do. Bobby is smart enough to make straight A's. He has a hard time getting his homework done, but he does apply himself doing his school work in class. Bobby takes his anger out on the other children. She knows he has problems with his dad drinking, but she's not sure what other problems he has at home. If she knew where his mom was, she'd get in touch with her about Bobby. None of the school staff can find her.

He ate his bread at lunch time, sitting away from the other kids so they would not see that he just had bread. He got water from the fountain.

'Nobody cares,' Bobby thought. 'I'm by myself and I have to get by as best I can. Someday I'll be old enough to leave this place and I'll have all the good stuff I want to eat. Surely I'm not bad 'cause I'm hungry and get something to eat any way I can. Someday soon, I will leave my dad 'cause he doesn't care anyway.'

Back at home, Bobby waits for his dad to come in with the groceries. His dad pulls up by the curb in his old car. Bobby goes out to help him carry in the groceries, but his dad gets out of the car and stumbles towards the house.

'He's drunk,' Bobby thought. 'And he didn't get us anything to eat.'

"Dad", Bobby said. "You didn't get the groceries today."

"Shut up kid!" Bart yelled. "I didn't feel like getting groceries! Fix what we've got"

Bobby looked in the kitchen cabinets. There are a couple of cans in the cabinet. One is chicken noodle soup and the other one is chili. He fixed the can of chili for them and gives his dad half of it in a bowl. His dad took a couple of bites from the bowl and then slings the bowl across the room.

"I ain't hungry anyway." he said to Bobby as he takes another drink from the bottle.

Bobby cleans up the floor. He eats part of the chili as he scoups it up. He said nothing, and then goes to his room. He lay down across his bed.

'Maybe I can find my Mom,' Bobby thought. 'She may still love me like she did when I was little.'

Tears began to roll down his face, but he made sure he was quiet so his Dad would not hear him. "Mom, mom,' Bobby thought, "I need you. Where are you Mom?'

"Bobby." A voice called. He looked around the room. He was afraid it was his Dad, but it didn't sound like his Dad. This voice is quiet and peaceful sounding.

"Bobby." The voice called again softly.

He looked around his room and saw a light in the corner. "Bobby." said a voice in the light.

The light came towards him and took the form of a person. The person stepped out of the light and stood at the foot of Bobby's bed. The young man has a bright light all around him that slowly dimmed and faded. He is the most handsome young man Bobby has ever seen. His hair is golden brown, long and wavy. He is wearing a white dress-like garment that comes to his knees and sparkles with silver as the young man moves. He has brown sandals on his feet and a silver sash around his waist. The young man smiled at Bobby and the man's brownish-gold eyes looked directly at Bobby. A wave of pure love flowed over the boy like a gentle breeze, and Bobby felt safe and even, peaceful.

In a calm voice Bobby asked, "Who are you? Are you an angel?"

Tears slid down Bobby's cheeks as he felt the love and acceptance from the presence before him. Bobby has never felt like this before.

"I am Andrew," he said. "I am here to help you and protect you."

"Why haven't you come before...before my Dad began hitting me? Why now?" Bobby studdered.

"I could not come before the right time," Andrew began to explain. "It is now time for things to change for you."

"What's going to change for me?" Bobby asked.

"I have watched over you all of your life, Bobby." Andrew said. "Some things I could not protect you from, but things could have been a lot worse than they were for you. I am here now because of your mother."

"My mother!" Bobby exclaimed. "Do you know my mother?"

"Yes, and she loves you very much and misses you." Andrew replied. "She is making plans to come for you, but do not tell your father for he may try to stop her."

"If my mother loves me, why did she leave?" Bobby asked.

"Your Mother left because your father treated her worse than he treats you." Andrew answered. "Your mom could not help you or herself while she was with your dad. She didn't want to leave you, but she had to get away to help herself before she could help you.

"Why hasn't she come to get me before now? It's been 3 years!" Bobby could not hold back the hurt in his voice. "My dad doesn't fix me anything to eat. I have to fix it myself. I have to beg money from my Dad to get milk, bread, cereal, soup and sandwich meat, 'cause some weeks he doesn't go to the store. Most days I have nothing for lunch at school. I take stuff from other kids 'cause I'm hungry all the time." Bobby says as tears stream down his face. "I have to wash my clothes and do everything. It's all my dad can do to just go to work, with his drinking. I'm always afraid my dad will lose his job. Then he'll be home all the time, and we won't have any money to buy food. Dad spends most of his money on alcohol. He stays mad at me all the time. Sometimes Dad is so mad, he hits me. I don't know why Dad is mad all the time."

"But you are not alone Bobby, I am always with you." Andrew said. "Your mom has to get strong enough to help herself first, then she can come back and get you. Your mom has a husband now and he's agreed with your mom to come and get you. They are working on the legal paperwork. When they come for you, you'll never have to go back to live with your Dad."

"When is my mom coming?" Bobby asked with excitement.

"It will be just a little while longer. Just know she is coming for you. So, just wait." Andrew said over his shoulder as he walked towards the corner of the room and disappeared in the light.

Bobby laid back down on the bed thinking about what Andrew told him. He will be glad when his Mom comes for him. An excitement is building up inside him as he thinks about it. He snuggles down in his covers and goes to sleep.

Saturday's should be a good day for kids since they are out of school. For Bobby, it is a whole day to keep away from his dad. This morning, his dad is not at home. Bobby looks to see what he can find to eat and opens a can of soup. He sits in the living room and watches TV. He's feeling somewhat peaceful knowing his mom is coming for him and his dad is not home. Then suddenly the door bursts open and his dad storms into the room cursing.

"He took my money that cheating son of a gun...." Bart yelled. He had been drinking and smelled of alcohol. "I was goin' to win some money, but that cheatin' dog got it."

"Dad," Bobby asked quietly. "Do you have any left to get us some food? We are out of nearly everything."

"I know that Bobby!" his dad yelled. "I wanted to get us some good stuff with the money I was goin' to win, but......." Bart went to cussing again.

"How much do you have dad, I'll walk to the store and get some stuff." Bobby asked, feeling more sorry for his dad than fearful.

"I've got $20.00." Bart said. "That has to do us a whole week."

Bobby hid the tears from his dad as Bart handed him the $20.00 bill. "I'll get all I can with this dad." He walked out the door thinking about what he can get that will last all week. Bread, peanut butter, Vienna sausage and potted meat; don't know if there will be enough for milk and cereal. Tears rolled down his face as he walked to the store.

'Andrew,' he thought. 'Please get me out of here soon.'

When he walked through the door at home with the groceries, his dad yelled at him.

"Fix me a sandwich!" Bart yelled. "Fix me two; I'm starving!"

"Dad, we've got to stretch it out all week so we'll have enough." Bobby said in a low voice.

"I don't care 'bout later, fix me something now!" Bart screamed at Bobby and slapped him hard on the back. Bobby got his balance and did not hit the floor.

"Just wait, dad, mom is coming for me soon and then I'll have plenty to eat!" Bobby yelled back at his dad from the kitchen. "And I'll be away from you!"

"What did you say boy?" his dad asked.

'Oh no', Bobby thought. 'I wasn't suppose to let him know about Mom coming for me.'

"Your mom ain't comin' for you boy. She doesn't care 'bout you." Bart yelled. "You're gonna stay right here and take care of your ol' dad. Don't you even think 'bout leavin' or I'll whip you good! Now fix me a sandwich!"

"Ok dad, whatever you say." Bobby replied trying to calm him down.

Bobby remembered that the church down the street is serving Thanksgiving meals today to the neighborhood. He slipped out the back door and ran down the street to the church. A nice lady asked him how many to-go plates did he need? Bobby saw an opportunity to get some food and said four. He carried the Styrofoam plates back to his house. As he walked into the door, he heard his dad yelling for him to bring his food. Bobby took him a plate of turkey and dressing and the fixings.

"Where did you get this?" Bart asked him as he opened up the plate. Bart wanted to be mad at him for getting the plate, but it smelled really good.

"I got them from the church down the street." Bobby said. "They were giving them away for Thanksgiving." Bart ate the food.

It was the best Thanksgiving meal they have had since before his mom left. The next morning is Thanksgiving Day. They each have a plate of food left from the day before. Bobby is thankful that his dad is calm for a change. His Dad is probably in a good mood because he has some good food to eat for a change. He sat in the living room with his Dad watching TV. His Dad is drinking, but he is quiet as he eats the Thanksgiving meal in the middle of the morning. Bobby is careful not to say or do anything to upset him. At about eleven o'clock, there is a knock at the door. Bart stumbled to the door and opened it. There stood a police officer with Cecelia.

"We've come for Bobby." the police officer said. Bobby ran to his room and got his duffle bag. Bobby was packed and ready to go. Bart cussed in the background as Bobby walked out the door. Bobby smiled. 'Thank-you, Andrew.' He thought. 'Thank-you.'

Printed in the United States
By Bookmasters